SPOTLIGHT
THE
COLD WAR

To Andy
(A pale shadow of its former self...
but anyway...)
Best wishes
from Nigel

Nigel Hunter

SPOTLIGHT ON HISTORY

Spotlight on the Age of Exploration and Discovery
Spotlight on the Age of Revolution
Spotlight on the Agricultural Revolution
Spotlight on the Cold War
Spotlight on the Collapse of Empires
Spotlight on Elizabethan England
Spotlight on the English Civil War
Spotlight on the First World War
Spotlight on the Industrial Revolution
Spotlight on Industry in the Twentieth Century
Spotlight on Medieval Europe
Spotlight on Post-War Europe
Spotlight on the Reformation
Spotlight on Renaissance Europe
Spotlight on the Rise of Modern China
Spotlight on the Russian Revolution
Spotlight on the Second World War
Spotlight on the Victorians

Cover illustration: **left:** The Kremlin, **right:** The White House.

First published in 1986 by Wayland (Publishers) Ltd
61 Western Road, Hove, East Sussex, BN3 1JD, England

© Copyright 1986 Wayland (Publishers) Ltd

British Library Cataloguing in Publication Data
Hunter, Nigel
    The cold war.—(Spotlight on history)
    1. World politics—1945- —Juvenile
    literature   2. Great powers—Juvenile
    literature
    I. Title   II. Series
    327   D840

    ISBN 0-85078-756-4

Typeset, printed and bound in the UK by The Bath Press, Avon

CONTENTS

1 ANOTHER KIND OF WARFARE

On the morning of 6 August 1945, the first atomic bomb, 'Little Boy', exploded over the Japanese city of Hiroshima. Tens of thousands of people were instantly incinerated in what appeared as 'a sheet of sun'. Others died beneath the rubble of blasted buildings, or in the ferocious fire-storm that followed. Dust and ashes turned day to night and the temperature fell to zero. Three days later a second atomic bomb, 'Fat Man', exploded over another Japanese city, Nagasaki, with similar devastating results. 'The war has developed not necessarily to the nation's advantage,' the Japanese Emperor, Hirohito, told his subjects. There was no alternative but for Japan to surrender, thus bringing the Second World War to an end.

Hiroshima, August 1945: the first city to be destroyed by a nuclear bomb.

Churchill, Roosevelt and Stalin at the Yalta Conference in 1945. The three leaders met to plan the final defeat and occupation of Nazi Germany and to decide upon the subsequent division of Europe.

Neither peace nor honour

'The power set free from the atom has changed everything,' said Albert Einstein, 'except our ways of thought'. The use of the atom bomb in August 1945 was not followed by peace, but another kind of warfare. From the beginning, this warfare was characterized as 'cold war', which basically means hostility between opposing forces that stops short of actual military conflict.

The earliest recorded use of the term is found in the writings of Don Juan Manuel (1282–1348). He wrote of the conflict between Christians and Muslims in fourteenth century Spain: 'War that is very strong and very hot ends either with death or peace, whereas cold war neither brings peace nor gives honour to the one who makes it.' The major opponents in the twentieth century Cold War have been the United States and the Soviet Union (USSR), who lead the world in nuclear weaponry. In so far as they have managed to avoid direct confrontation 'cold war' is an apt description of their relations. Nuclear war would be much stronger and infinitely hotter than anything Don

Juan Manuel might have imagined, six centuries ago. He might not even have recognized it as war. But his comment that cold war 'neither brings peace nor gives honour' to those who make it, still rings true.

Nevertheless, the term is somewhat misleading, since within the framework of the Cold War there have been many armed confrontations in various parts of the world. Directly or indirectly, the major powers have always been involved. It has been a conflict of ideologies, of competing political and economic systems and rival power-blocs of nations. Capitalism and communism, the two opposing forms of government and society have been struggling for supremacy.

The challenge of communism
Communist theory originated in the writings of Karl Marx (1818–83). Marx's analysis of nineteenth century industrial society led him to believe that revolutionary change was inevitable. In the capitalist system, as he called it, the 'means of production' were owned by the few people whose private wealth derived from the exploitation of those who worked for them. The result, for the mass of people, was misery. To Marx, the dynamic of historical change lay in class struggle. The transition to a society which would be free from material want would begin with a revolutionary 'dictatorship of the proletariat (industrial working class).' At this stage, which Marx defined as socialism, the means of production would pass into state ownership. Eventually, a classless society would emerge, and production and distribution of goods would take place on the principle, 'From each according to his ability, to each according to his needs'. This would be communism.

No state has as yet managed to achieve full communism. It remains an ideal, possibly never to be realized. If the USSR is called a communist state, it is because it is led by the Communist Party. Its *aim*, rather than its achievement, is communism.

From the time of the Bolshevik Revolution in Russia in 1917, the Soviet state and the capitalist nations, especially the United States and Britain, have been locked into a relationship of mutual antagonism. Bolshevism, renamed 'communism' shortly after the Revolution, was described by the US Secretary of State in 1918, as 'the most hideous and monstrous thing that the human mind has ever conceived.' It aimed 'to make the ignorant and incapable mass of humanity dominant on the earth.' Gripped by a 'Red Scare' of major proportions, the Western powers intervened militarily to try to overthrow the Bolshevik Revolution, but they failed.

The immense radioactive dust cloud of a nuclear explosion.

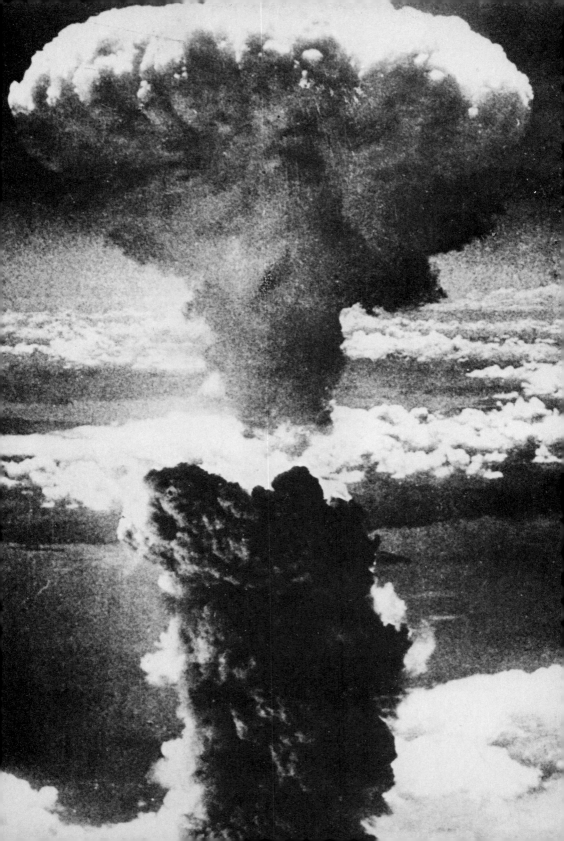

Karl Marx (1818–83), the founder of modern Communism. With Friedrich Engels, he wrote The Communist Manifesto *in 1848.*

Under the leadership of Joseph Stalin from 1927 to 1953, the USSR grew to the status of a world power, but his efforts to create 'socialism in one country' proved ruthless in the extreme. Millions of 'class enemies', those people opposed to Stalin's methods and ideology, were imprisoned, executed or exiled. Stalin, more than anyone else, gave communism a bad name in the West. Only the existence of a common enemy, Adolf Hitler, could have made allies of the Western powers and the USSR during the Second World War. With the defeat of fascism in 1945, the old antagonisms re-emerged in a more intensified form.

8

The atomic bomb

The American scientist Robert Oppenheimer, who helped develop the atomic bomb, was present at the first test explosion in 1944. 'A few people laughed, a few people cried. Most people were silent,' he recalled. 'I remembered the line from the Hindu scripture, the *Bhagavad Gita*: . . . "Now I am become death, destroyer of worlds."' With the atomic bomb an unprecedented, immense and horrifying power had been unleashed. The first demonstration of its destructive power came at the Japanese cities of Hiroshima and Nagasaki. The question now was, could this source of power ever be controlled? Or, like Frankenstein's monster, might it grow to threaten everything its creator most valued, which, in this case, was the fabric of life itself?

Robert Oppenheimer, director of the wartime 'Manhattan Project' which first developed nuclear weapons.

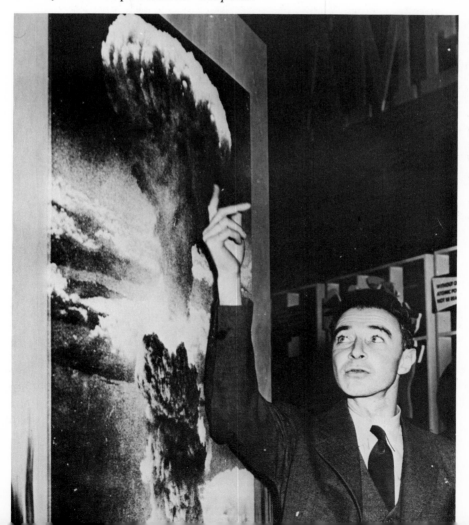

Among the international flags of the Veterans' War Memorial Building in San Francisco, the Earl of Halifax, British Ambassador to the United States, signs the UN charter. It was the birth of the United Nations.

The bomb was the first-ever subject of debate by the United Nations Organization (UN), which was formed in 1945 to promote peace and unity among the nations of the world. Already, the prospect of an 'armament race of a rather desperate character' was being debated. At this stage all the atomic expertise was in the United States, and it seemed likely that the Soviet Union would attempt to catch up. Subsequent US proposals for international control of atomic energy seemed, to the USSR, designed to maintain the American advantage, and to amount to unacceptable outside interference in Soviet affairs. The Soviet counter-proposal was simpler and more in line with the original, unanimously-accepted, UN resolution, which was to destroy all existing nuclear weapons and ban their future production. But just two weeks later, in a test at Bikini Atoll in the Pacific, the USA exploded a fourth bomb, and agreement on an outright ban receded into the indefinite future. In 1949, thanks in part to information gained through espionage, the USSR exploded its first atomic bomb. With ever increasing destructive power the nuclear arms race was on.

In theory, the threat of a 'nuclear exchange', has prevented war between the major powers. But paradoxically, this in itself has allowed them to become more warlike. To some extent, the Cold War has been an exercise in brinkmanship to see just how far either side can go before someone 'presses the button'.

2 POST-WAR HOSTILITIES

Towards the end of the Second World War, amidst the wreckage of the 'Thousand Year Reich' in Germany, Hitler gave a thought to future US–Soviet relations. He predicted that, 'The laws of both history and geography will compel these two nations to a trial of strength either militarily or in the fields of economics and ideology.' The European power-vacuum created by the defeat of Nazi Germany provided the first testing-ground in the Cold War.

Joseph Stalin, the dictatorial leader of the USSR from 1927, who created a totalitarian state, crushing all opposition.

CHAIRMAN

Marshal Tito (1892–1965), leader of Yugoslavia from 1945, who practised communism while remaining independent from the Soviet bloc.

Spheres of influence

Through a series of wartime agreements between the Allies, France, Britain, the USA and the USSR, preliminary 'spheres of influence' in Europe had already begun to take shape. The Soviet Union had suffered twenty million fatalities, and came very close to defeat, during the war. Now, to ensure there would not be another invasion from the West, Stalin intended to create a 'buffer-zone' of non-hostile nations on his country's eastern borders. In Bulgaria, Rumania, Hungary, Czechoslovakia, and Poland, all liberated from the Nazis by the Soviet Red Army, pro-Soviet governments were soon in power. The US ambassador to Moscow informed President Harry Truman (1945–52), that a 'barbarian invasion of Europe' was under way: 'Soviet control over any foreign country did not mean merely influence on their foreign relations but the extension of the Soviet system with secret police, extinction of freedom of speech, etc.' Stalin's view, if cynical, was less one-sided: 'Everyone imposes his own system as far as his army has the power to do so,' he claimed.

Germany and Austria were divided into four 'occupation zones', with power shared between the governments of the USA, Britain, France and the USSR. The principal cities, Berlin and Vienna, were likewise divided, becoming enclaves of Western influence within Soviet-occupied territory. The leaders of both Yugoslavia and Albania, Tito and Hoxha, were ex-partisans who had gained national liberation with little help from Stalin and formed more independent communist governments. The lines of division were drawn between East and West. In a famous speech from the US President's home state of Missouri in 1946, the British war-time Prime Minister, Winston Churchill, alleged that 'an iron curtain has descended across the continent' and that

> 'Communist fifth columns are established and work in complete unity and absolute obedience to the directions they receive from the Communist centre.'

'Mr Churchill now takes the stand of the warmongers,' Stalin commented, 'and in this Mr Churchill is not alone.'

Winston Churchill (1874–1965), British Prime Minister during the Second World War, and between 1951 and 1955.

Harry S. Truman (1884–1972), US President 1945–53, who approved the dropping of the two atom bombs on Japan.

Containment

The 'Truman Doctrine' and the 'Marshall Plan' of 1947 were Western policies of 'containment', intended to counter 'the natural and instinctive urges of Russian rulers' to want to expand Russian power. 'The free peoples of the world look to us for support in maintaining their freedom,' President Truman announced. Economic difficulties had forced Britain to withdraw its aid to the royalist government in Greece, which was fighting a civil war against what the West considered to be 'Communist insurgents.' The Truman Doctrine, which promised military aid to countries threatened by communism first took effect with the substitution of American for British support in Greece. But from the vantage-point of twenty years, one US politician admitted in 1967: 'We had to back not the good guys but the bad guys in Greece. . . . We did not back the people. We backed the monarchy.' An old Greek shepherd pleaded in 1947, 'What is to be said when "outlaws" are more law-abiding than the government, and behave to us more decently?'

Physically undamaged by the war, the USA was the wealthiest nation in the world. The Marshall Plan was proposed by General Marshall, (US Secretary of State 1945–7), and consisted of the offer of American credits and aid to Europe: 'Our policy is directed not against any country or doctrine, but against hunger, poverty, desperation, and chaos', claimed General Marshall. 'Its purpose should be the revival of a working economy in the world so as to permit the emergence of political and social conditions in which free institutions can exist.' Later he confirmed that the USSR and eastern European countries were included in the offer. This was viewed by *Pravda*, the official Soviet newspaper, as 'a plan for political pressure with the help of dollars, a plan for interference in the domestic affairs of other countries'. On such grounds, the USSR eventually rejected Marshall Aid, and neighbouring countries were obliged to follow suit.

The Berlin blockade
The Communist Information Bureau, or 'Cominform', claimed that the Marshall Plan was aimed at 'the enslavement of Europe' through American capitalism. Widespread strikes in France and Italy appeared to be evidence of a Soviet-inspired bid to undermine the American-backed European Recovery Programme. If so, it failed, and among the sixteen nations which received Marshall Aid, economic renewal proceded apace. In the years that followed in Western Europe, the American 'Open Door' policy of free trade would prevail. In Eastern

Germans gather together their belongings as they wait for evacuation by air during the Berlin blockade.

A Soviet tank disperses demonstrators in East Berlin. The protests were against the declaration of martial law by the authorities.

Europe, there would be planned economies following the Soviet model.

Four-power agreement by the Allies on the future of Germany proved impossible to reach. By the spring of 1948, the USA, Britain and France had decided to develop the country's western zones as a separate economic and political entity. The first step was the introduction of a new West German currency, and this was promptly countered

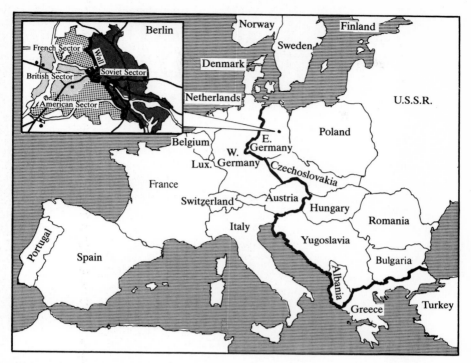

Post-war Europe, showing the East–West divide between Communist and non-Communist nations.

by the introduction of a new East German currency. The dispute between the Western powers and the USSR came to centre on Berlin, the divided city. Already, the Soviets had begun to restrict Western access to Berlin, which involved crossing Germany's eastern, Soviet sector. Before long all road and rail links were closed. According to Truman, 'What the Russians were trying to do was to get us out of Berlin.' The blockade, and the subsequent airlift of supplies by the Western allies to the two million inhabitants of West Berlin, continued for almost a year, until eventually the Soviet side yielded and normal traffic was resumed. 'We demonstrated to the people of Europe that with their co-operation we would act and act resolutely when their freedom was threatened,' Truman declared.

Within months of the crisis ending, two new German states had been established, the western German Federal Republic (FDR) and the eastern German Democratic Republic (DDR). With the last vestiges of non-Communist participation in East-European governments now gone, Europe was irrevocably split into two mutually antagonistic blocs.

17

3 IN THE THIRD WORLD

While Europe was undergoing division, events with far-reaching consequences were taking place on the other side of the world. China had been experiencing civil war for almost twenty years. The war ended in 1949, with victory going to the communist forces led by Mao Tse-tung. The world's most populous state became a 'People's Republic'. The success of Mao's peasant army proved that communist revolution was possible, not only in the advanced industrial nations, as proposed by classical Marxist theory, but also in the under-developed, mainly rural countries of the 'Third World'. It also meant that there was a second communist 'giant', China, confronting the capitalist nations of the West.

Mao Tse-tung (1893–1976), the Chinese Marxist statesman, who founded the People's Republic of China in 1949.

The Korean War

After the Second World War, China's neighbour Korea had been occupied and divided by the USSR and the USA. Prior to the withdrawal of these forces, two rival governments had come to power. In the north, there was a communist regime, whilst in the south, following UN-supervised elections, there was an anti-communist regime. Both governments claimed sovereignty over the whole country. To some extent, the situation was similar to that in Germany.

In January 1950, the US Secretary of State, Dean Acheson, defined the American 'defensive perimeter' in the Pacific in such a way as to suggest that the integrity of South Korea was not a particularly vital concern. To the North Koreans, this amounted almost to an invitation to invade the South, and in June, equipped with military supplies from the USSR, they attacked. The USA immediately responded, sending air, sea and ground forces to support the South. And under the patronage of the United Nations, troops from seventeen other countries eventually joined them. 'We do not want the fighting in Korea to expand into a general war,' President Truman proclaimed. 'It will not spread unless communist imperialism draws other armies and governments into the fight of the aggressors against the United Nations.'

However, whereas the original intention had been merely to restore the status quo, it soon became the aim of the US and the UN to reunite Korea as a non-communist state. At this point, China intervened, sending hundreds of thousands of troops to support the North Koreans. Some US military personnel called for attacks against China and even for the use of nuclear weapons. But more level-headed opinions prevailed. The Chairman of the American Joint Chiefs of Staff said, 'Red China is not the most powerful nation seeking to dominate the world. Frankly ... this strategy would involve us in the wrong war, at the wrong place, at the wrong time, and with the wrong enemy.' Ultimately, in 1953, the old north–south borders were restored at a total cost of 3,500,000 lives. China, however, had entered the arena of world politics.

Colonial conflict

A major feature of the post-war period was the collapse of the old colonial empires. Almost inevitably, this entailed a considerable degree of military conflict. Many nationalist movements sought not only to bring independence to their countries, but also to replace the old regimes with governments of a specifically socialist, or communist, character. In South and South East Asia, such movements often took their inspiration from the example of Mao's revolution in China, and employed similar tactics of guerrilla warfare.

An American soldier interrogates a Korean nurse during the Korean War. The war was fought between North Korea, aided by Communist China, and South Korea, supported by the US.

The anti-communist campaign by the British in Malaya in the 1950s was conducted with ruthless efficiency. Wholesale transference of the local Chinese population into 'new villages' surrounded by barbed wire and armed guards prevented the mainly Chinese guerrillas from establishing contact with their potential supporters. This, together with bombing campaigns against guerrilla camps, forays into the jungle on what were called 'search and destroy' missions, and strict reprisals against sympathizers, broke the back of the movement. The minority anti-communist and more privileged Malay population assisted the British and were assured a leading role in the post-independence era. When the British withdrew, in 1957, the 'communist menace' in Malaya had been defeated.

British soldiers in Malaya attach a rocket projectile to the wing of an aircraft in preparation for attack.

Vietnam was another story. Here, as in neighbouring Laos and Cambodia, the colonial power was France. The French leader, Charles de Gaulle, had made his position clear in 1944: 'The attainment of self-government in the colonies—even in the most distant future—must be excluded.' France, however, was by no means invincible. Ho Chi Minh, a Western-educated communist who was based in the northern part of Vietnam, was in control of a popular and highly motivated guerrilla force, the Vietminh, which was prepared to wage as long a war as necessary to rid the country of foreign domination. In 1954, at the French base of Dien Bien Phu, the Vietminh, backed by both the Chinese and Soviets, inflicted a decisive defeat on the American-backed French forces. However, with the subsequent partitioning of Vietnam and increasing US involvement, full independence as a communist state was still two decades away.

President Ho Chi Minh (1892–1969), the Vietnamese nationalist leader, with some of his younger compatriots.

Fidel Castro (right) and Che Guevara (left) make a triumphant entry into Havana.

The Cuban Revolution

In November 1956, a small vessel called the *Granma* left the coast of Mexico, heading for Cuba. Aboard were eighty-two revolutionaries under the leadership of Fidel Castro. Just a fortnight later, three days after landing, all but twelve were dead. It was not a favourable beginning to one of the most significant events of the period, the Cuban Revolution.

For well over a century, the United States had been the dominant power in the Western hemisphere. Many of the dictatorships and military regimes in Central and South America were under US patronage. The region was considered 'Uncle Sam's (US) backyard'. Economic exploitation had reduced many countries to conditions of outright poverty. Rule by corrupt, oppressive and dictatorial regimes, often

23

Tanks of Fidel Castro's army roll past streets lined with cheering crowds, on their way to downtown Havana, 8 January, 1959.

backed by the USA, resulted for the mass of people in day-to-day insecurity and resentment. In each country, there was an elite who profited by these arrangements, and in whose interest it was that they continued. Cuba was ruled by a military dictator named Batista. Its capital, Havana, was an exotic 'playground' for wealthy Americans, and a city where the Mafia had considerable investments. At that time most of the Cuban population was very poor and had no say in the running of their country. It was for them that the Revolution was fought.

After their initial defeat, the guerrillas managed to regroup, and gradually to make progress. Winning the 'hearts and minds of the people', their numbers increased until they were unstoppable, and after two years' fighting, they marched triumphantly into the capital, Havana. 'If all Latin American peoples should raise the flag of dignity, as Cuba has done, monopoly would tremble; it would have to accommodate to a new political-economic situation and to substantial profits,' wrote the guerrilla leader Che Guevara, who was instrumental in Castro's victory. The Revolution answered the 'urgent demands of a people that wishes to be free, . . . to be master of its economy, . . . to prosper and to reach ever higher goals of social development.' Inaccurately labelling the Revolution 'Communist', the US began to apply pressure, the consequences of which proved to be alarming.

4 SECURITY AND SUBVERSION

In the West, interest began to turn to concern for internal security. In his 'iron curtain' speech of 1946, Winston Churchill had called the public's attention to 'communist fifth columns' working under the direction of Moscow for the subversion of Western governments. Subsequently, in the USA, a virulent campaign against known communists began to take place. It was applied mainly to individuals in public life, to government officials, and to workers in the entertainments industry. In time, this became known as the 'McCarthy period' after Senator Joe McCarthy, who built an unparalleled reputation as an anti-communist 'witch-hunter'.

Joe McCarthy (left), US Republican senator who led the notorious post-war anti-Communist 'witch hunts'.

Naming names

In 1947 the House Un-American Activities Committee (HUAC) began its investigations in Hollywood. 'Hundreds of very prominent film capital people have been named as Communists to us,' one of its members claimed. It was alleged that the Screen Writers Guild, in particular, was 'lousy with Communists'. Those called to testify were divided into two groups: the 'friendly' and 'unfriendly' witnesses. To the 'unfriendlies' and their supporters, who disagreed with McCarthy's witch-hunt, what was taking place constituted 'an alarming trend to control the cultural life of the American people in accordance with reactionary conceptions of our national interest.' It was an 'assault on civil liberties', and on the constitutionally guaranteed right to freedom of speech. The HUAC, they claimed, was 'an instrument of political repression' whose goal was 'control of the film industry through intimidation.' 'We do not believe the Committee is conducting a fair investigation,' the *New York Times* commented. 'We think the course on which it

Facing the Inquisitors: an HUAC hearing of the early 1950s, chaired by Senator Joe McCarthy.

Film stars in the courtroom: among several whose careers were threatened were Danny Kaye (middle row, left) and Humphrey Bogart (centre, right).

is embarked threatens to lead to greater dangers than those with which it is presently concerned.'

Ten of those who had been 'named' as communists by the 'friendly' witnesses resolutely refused to confirm or deny the insistently repeated question, 'Are you now or have you ever been a member of the Communist Party?' This question was perceived as unconstitutional pressure to reveal political opinions. Wrote Ring Lardner Jr, one of those questioned:

'Everything I know about the history of inquisitions and test oaths confirms my conviction that there is only a minor difference between forcing a man to say what his opinions are and dictating what his opinions should be. Whenever men have been compelled to open their minds to government authority, men's minds have ceased to be free.'

However, the right to ask the question had been upheld by an appeal-court judge, whose reasoning reflected the wider context of the issue:

'. . . the destiny of all nations hangs in the balance in the current ideological struggle between communistic-thinking and democratic-

An anti-Soviet demonstration outside the UN headquarters in New York. The demonstrators are carrying placards and posters which implicate the Soviets in the death of Dag Hammarskjold, the UN Secretary-General.

thinking peoples .. It is ... beyond dispute that the motion picture industry plays a critically important role in the moulding of public opinion and that motion pictures are, or are capable of being, a potent medium of propaganda dissemination which may influence the minds of millions of American people.'

The 'Hollywood Ten' were convicted for contempt of court and sent to prison for a year. 'If we lose,' one of them had warned, 'then it will be a dark, dark time for free thought, free speech and free culture in America.'

The blacklists

What followed were semi-official 'blacklists' of ideologically 'unreliable' Americans. By law, union leaders and public employees had to sign oaths of loyalty to the United States and to disown any connection with the Communist Party or affiliated groups. As many as 60,000 people were blacklisted, which meant they were liable to lose their jobs, and were subjected to public contempt and social ostracism. 'Reds under the beds' became a familiar term for supposed subversives (those likely to overthrow the government). 'Red-baiting' was rife, with smear tactics being applied against anybody remotely connected with radical or liberal causes. At HUAC hearings, the pressure to inform on colleagues, friends and acquaintances was overwhelming.

Film director Joseph Losey commented that: 'The most terrifying thing about the atmosphere was seeing people succumb, and seeing all protest disappear. Because if you did protest, you'd had it.' Like a number of those on the blacklist, Losey went into exile so as to be able to continue working. Many more were not so fortunate, as the State Department withheld or annulled their passports. As for Hollywood itself, it soon began to turn out 'Cold War movies'— propaganda films with such titles as *I Married a Communist*, *I Was a Communist for the FBI*, *The Red Menace*, *Red Snow*, *Red Planet Mars*, *The Iron Curtain*.

The 'Red Scare' maintained its momentum until the mid 1950s. While the leaders of the American Communist Party were convicted of conspiring 'knowingly and wilfully to advocate and teach the duty and necessity of overthrowing and destroying the Government of the United States by force and violence', most of those caught in the McCarthy 'net' were, in all likelihood, basically loyal citizens. The dangers they posed to state security were certainly exaggerated.

Spies in high places

In the early 1950s espionage had given cause for genuine concern. The Soviet Union's first test explosion of an atomic bomb, in 1949, had been achieved considerably earlier than most experts had predicted. In 1950, a German physicist named Klaus Fuchs was arrested in London and charged with spying for the USSR. As a refugee from Nazi Germany, Fuchs had worked first in Britain and then, during the war, on secret atomic research in the USA. Despite his communist record, the British had given him security clearance, merely extracting a promise that he would relinquish his contact with communist groups while occupied with this work. In fact, he began to pass secret information almost at once. News of his subsequent confession caused consternation to former colleagues: 'There he was, this spy, standing right at the centre of what we believed at the time to be the world's greatest

Julius and Ethel Rosenberg, who paid the ultimate penalty for spying for the Soviets. A question mark, however, hangs over their guilt.

secret.' One leading scientist assessed the damage thus: 'There was much ... that they could have established for themselves, but for a power in a hurry, it was of measureless value....' After serving nine years in prison, Fuchs returned to East Germany to pursue his career in nuclear research.

Two Americans convicted of spying for the Soviets, Julius and Ethel Rosenburg, paid the ultimate penalty in the United States in 1953. Despite an international campaign for clemency based on doubts concerning their guilt, they were executed.

Perhaps the most notorious case was that of Britons Donald Maclean, Guy Burgess and Kim Philby. They had been recruited into the Soviet spy network while students at Cambridge University during the 1930s. Like many people at the time, including most of the Americans 'exposed' during the McCarthy period, they had been convinced that communism offered the strongest source of opposition to fascism. They worked undiscovered as 'double agents' for many years, rising to positions of trust and responsibility within the British diplomatic and intelligence services. Through their work at the Washington Embassy, Maclean and Burgess had access to secrets of a political and military nature. Combined with the details provided by Fuchs, the strategical information received through Burgess and Maclean gave the Soviets a valuable overview of Western policy. When Philby, who worked as a liaison officer between the British and American secret services, discovered in 1951 that Maclean was being investigated by the FBI (the US government investigation agency), he alerted Burgess. Burgess helped Maclean to escape to Moscow, and he himself defected soon after. The shock waves continued to vibrate for many years to come.

Guy Burgess, the British diplomat and Soviet spy who defected to Moscow with Donald Maclean in 1951.

5 MILITARY MANOEUVRES

In 1949 President Truman initiated moves to 'strengthen freedom-loving nations against the dangers of aggression'. The North Atlantic Treaty Organization (NATO) established a military alliance between the USA, ten European countries and Canada. Anticipating the signing, the Soviet Foreign Ministry protested: 'The aims of the Alliance ... are interwoven with ... plans for the establishment of Anglo-American world supremacy under the aegis (sponsorship) of the USA.' NATO was said by the West to be solely defensive. 'Peace through strength' was the strategy, strength to deter attack, and to negotiate problems 'without fear'.

The signing of the North Atlantic Treaty (NATO) in 1949. NATO is an international organization established for purposes of collective security.

Dwight D. Eisenhower (1890–1969), US general and Republican statesman, who was President of the USA between 1953 and 1961.

Testing developments

With members of the US Airforce stationed in Britain and with US troops under NATO command on the continent, Western Europe came under the 'protection' of the American nuclear 'umbrella'. The USSR continued its research into nuclear weapons, despite favouring an 'absolute prohibition' of their use. And the USA within the context of its 'programme for peace and security', pursued a new project—the 'super-bomb'.

NATO forces were based near the West German border in 1950 to counter a possible threat from the East. 'It was felt that the Korean War was only a curtain-raiser to a Russian-sponsored war of unification in Germany', a British officer recalled. The West German Chancellor spoke of the well-armed East German militia, and the Soviet troops reportedly ready to back them up. Germany's long-term future seemed an intractable problem. Whereas Soviet diplomats pressed for a re-united, disarmed neutral Germany, the leading Western Allies favoured West German re-armament as a partner within NATO, with reunification to follow.

In October 1952, Britain became the world's third nuclear power, after exploding an atom bomb in the Monte Bello Islands off Australia's western coast. The following month, the USA tested a hydrogen device, with an explosive force eight times stronger than the bomb that obliterated Hiroshima. That November, Dwight D. Eisenhower, formerly

33

Nikita Khrushchev, Premier of the Soviet Union (1958–64). As Premier, he pursued a policy of peaceful co-existence with the West.

Supreme Commander of NATO, was elected President of the USA. With the death of Stalin in March 1953, East–West relations entered a new phase, although initial hopes for a 'thaw' soon faded. In June, the workers of East Berlin rose against the Communist Party government, which was calling for higher levels of productivity. The revolt began with a strike and a march on the Economics Ministry and it ended with the 'People's Police' and Soviet tanks firing into crowds on the streets. Order was restored, but it was not the last event of its kind. In August 1953 it was reported that the USSR, like the US the year before, had tested a hydrogen weapon.

A new man in the Kremlin

The new United States President, Eisenhower, demanded concrete 'deeds' or action from the USSR, to prove the sincerity of its public claim to be peaceable. He also pressed hard for West German re-armament. When a satisfactory formula for limitation and control of arms had been reached, in May 1955, West Germany became a member of NATO. Within a week, Eastern-bloc countries signed the treaty of the Warsaw Pact, which established a military alliance between the USSR and its 'satellite' states (states dependent upon the USSR for economic support and political direction). This appeared to be a demonstration of strength and unity yet the next day the Soviet Union signed the Austrian State Treaty which seemed to involve giving way on some issues, and to answer the US President's call for 'deeds'. All four powers withdrew their occupation forces from West Germany, and the country became a non-aligned state.

Nikita Khrushchev had emerged as the new Soviet First Secretary in 1958. Following several years of hostility, friendly relations between the USSR and Yugoslavia were resumed. Tito, Prime Minister of Yugoslavia between 1945 and 1953, had been criticized by the USSR for his 'revisionist' policies. He had asserted his independence from Moscow by making his own interpretation of communism and had also cultivated relations with the West. Khrushchev now admitted that in the past there had been Soviet 'errors' in the relationship between the two countries.

At the four-power summit conference of July 1955, an agreement on Germany was signed by the USA, USSR, Britain and France: '...unification of Germany will be carried out in conformity with the national interests of the German people and in the interests of European security.' But this was an indefinite commitment that solved nothing. Two months later, the USSR established diplomatic relations with West Germany, and gave up their control of East Germany's foreign policy. This, in effect, was an official recognition of Germany's division. But East Germany, the DDR, was recognized only by other

Communist governments. West Germany, the FDR, continued to claim sovereignty over the country as a whole.

According to Marxist–Leninist theory, wars that are caused by 'imperialist aggression' are inevitable, until the final victory of communism. But 'present-day conditions,' said Khrushchev in February 1956, demanded 'peaceful co-existence': 'either peaceful co-existence or the most destructive war in history. There is no third way ... The method of negotiation must become the sole method of solving international problems.' He also denounced Stalin for having enforced rule through terror and for acting with 'suspicion and haughtiness ... to whole parties and nations.' In 1956, the Soviet Twentieth Party Congress proclaimed that 'the full sovereignty of each socialist state' would be the basic understanding on which future relations between the USSR and its East European neighbours would be built.

A Squadron of Soviet tanks reimpose order in East Berlin after the workers' uprising of 1953.

Some of the 5,000 refugees from Soviet occupied Germany who flocked to the West Berlin registration offices to seek asylum in the Western sectors of the divided city.

Hungary and Suez, 1956

Any hopes that the Cold War was coming to an end were confounded later that year, by events in the Middle East and in Hungary. In July 1956, President Nasser of Egypt nationalized (put under state control) the Suez Canal, taking control of French and British investments. The British Prime Minister, Sir Anthony Eden, claimed that the USSR was 'using Nasser, with or without his knowledge, to further its own aims'. As negotiations started, Britain, France and Israel prepared for military action.

Popular revolt against the Soviet-backed government in Hungary began with a nationalist demonstration on 23 October 1956. 'We want an independent national policy based on the principle of socialism', declared the President of the Writers' Association. 'Our relations with all countries ... should be regulated on the basis of the principle of equality.' A gigantic statue of Stalin was toppled over by the crowd. 'Hilarious laughter and uproarious applause greeted the fall of the tyrant,' an emigré writer, George Mikas, later recalled. The arrival of Soviet tanks provoked widening unrest. 'I feel with the Hungarian people', President Eisenhower said, but Western involvement was limited to propaganda by radio. The Soviets agreed to a new Hungarian government even though it contained two non-communists, and the USSR announced it would withdraw its troops 'as soon as the Hungarian government finds it necessary.'

British officers hold a ceremony in Egypt, when along with French and Israeli troops, they fought the Egyptians for control of the Suez Canal.

*Three temporary graves in a street in Budapest, when in the autumn
of 1956, after anti-Communist feeling led to increasing disturbances,
Soviet troops fired at protesting civilians.*

It soon became clear, however, that Hungary was about to declare
its neutrality, to leave the Warsaw Pact and allow political freedom
to non-Communist parties. Anti-communist feeling led to increasing
disturbances. To the USSR, complete 'counter-revolution' was intoler-
able. On 4 November, a full-scale military attack was launched. The
people fought against the Soviet forces 'practically until the last Hungarian bullet had been fired and long after all hope had been given
up.' But Western protests were weakened by simultaneous action in
Egypt. On 5 November, British and French forces invaded Egypt in
support of Israeli troops who had attacked the previous week. American pressure for Anglo-French withdrawal was intense, as the US
believed the invasion could result in increased Soviet influence in the
region. The USSR, for its part, referred ominously to 'rocket tech-
niques' that could be used against Britain. Within twenty-four hours,
the invasion was abandoned. For the West, it was a political disaster.
Khrushchev claimed an improvement of Soviet prestige over Suez,
taking credit for ending the crisis. But over Hungary, where 30,000
patriots died in the uprising, Soviet prestige was permanently damaged.

39

6 TO THE BRINK— AND BEYOND

The Berlin Wall has become a symbol of the Cold War. Bleak and foreboding, surmounted by watchtowers and armed guards, it divides the city in two. It was built, the then East German leader, Walter Ulbricht, explained, because the West German government had fallen 'into the hands of Fascists, Nazis, militarists, revanchists, warmongers, slave-traders and head-hunters'. Ostensibly, the Wall was there to keep out spies and saboteurs. The fact that it also kept the East Germans in was not officially mentioned. The construction of the Wall, in 1961, followed three years of revived controversy over the city's future status.

The Brandenburger Tor in Berlin, an East–West crossing point. The ideological and physical division of Europe was centred in Berlin, a city divided between East and West.

Walter Ulbricht, who was largely responsible for the establishment and development of East German Communism.

The Berlin crisis

At the end of 1958, Khrushchev had called on the Western powers 'to renounce the remnants of the occupation regime in Berlin and thereby make it possible to create a normal situation in the capital of the (East) German Democratic Republic.' In a note that spoke of Berlin as 'a smouldering fuse that has been connected to a powder keg', the USSR added a time limit. This time limit meant that after six months, control of the access routes to West Berlin, which were then still in Soviet hands, would be transferred to the East German authorities. But the Western allies did not officially recognize the DDR. Discussion over access to Berlin would, effectively, force recognition; not to do so might result in military confrontation on the East German *autobahns*

The former British Conservative Prime Minister Harold Macmillan (1957–63), who visited Moscow in February 1959.

(motorways). A major crisis threatened.

Harold Macmillan, the British Prime Minister between 1957 and 1963 emphasized the dangers of the situation when he visited Moscow in February 1959. The tension seemed to ease, as the six months' deadline was withdrawn and Khrushchev conceded Western 'rights for their stay in Berlin.' In September, Khrushchev visited the USA, returning with the firm belief that Eisenhower 'sincerely wants, like us, to end the Cold War.'

A full-scale summit meeting arranged for May 1960, however, never took place. On 1 May, an American U2 spy-plane was shot down over the USSR. President Eisenhower refused publicly to apologise for the infringement of Soviet air space, and the summit was called off. Another summit, in June 1961, did take place, involving Khrushchev and the new US President, John F. Kennedy. However, on the main issues of Berlin and nuclear weapons, they failed to reach an agreement.

As tension mounted once again, tens of thousands of East Germans were crossing to the West, via Berlin. For a state with substantial economic problems, the continuing loss of manpower (2,000,000 or more since 1949) was unacceptable. Following a Warsaw Pact meeting, the East Germans began to build the Berlin Wall. Those who have tried to cross it since, have had to dodge bullets and mines to succeed, and many have died in the attempt. But West Berlin remained under Allied control and the USSR kept charge of the access routes. A military confrontation, at least, had been avoided.

Western troops on one side and East German troops on the other of the recently constructed Berlin Wall (1961). The activity was at the Friedrichstrasse cross point.

US President John F. Kennedy addresses a huge rally in front of the City Hall in Berlin, in June 1963.

The Cuban missile crisis

The Berlin question caused considerable dangers of war. During the Cuban missile crisis of October 1962, however, the world came even closer to 'the abyss of destruction', according to President John F. Kennedy. Following the Revolution, and the subsequent nationalization of American investments, Cuba had been subjected to an economic boycott by the USA. Prime Minister Castro consequently turned to the USSR for trade links and for aid. In April 1961, the US gave its backing to an invasion of Cuba by a force of anti-Castro exiles, whose defeat, at the Bay of Pigs, was immediate and total. For the USA, this was a disastrous episode. Also, since it seemed quite possible that a second attempt might follow, it led to increased military co-operation between Cuba and the USSR.

In mid-October 1962, American spy-planes photographed a number of Soviet nuclear missiles being installed in Cuba, just ninety miles from the US coast. This meant they could hit their targets in less than two minutes. To the Soviet Union, the emplacement of missiles in Cuba partly compensated for the United States' overall nuclear superiority. To President Kennedy, they represented a 'clandestine, reckless

44

Bodies lie strewn in the road in Saigon. South Vietnamese soldiers drag one away in a sheet after bloody battles between the Viet Cong and South Vietnamese and American troops, in January 1968.

and provocative threat to world peace'. 'This is the week when I had better earn my salary', he told an aide. An airstrike against the missile silos was considered, as was a full-scale invasion. But either might easily have led to war with the USSR. Kennedy decided on a preliminary blockade of the island. Soviet shipping heading for Cuba would be stopped and turned back. Meanwhile, an invasion force would be prepared, and intense political pressure for the withdrawal of the missiles would be applied.

The Soviet leader, Khrushchev, in turn, accused Kennedy of 'recklessly playing with nuclear fires'. With nuclear forces on 'red alert', the situation was extremely tense. Then, on 26 and 27 October, two contradictory messages reached Washington. The first, from Khrushchev, offered to remove the missiles if the US would undertake not to invade Cuba. But before Kennedy could reply to this, the second message arrived, from the Soviet Presidium. This, which was much less acceptable, demanded the removal of US missiles from Turkey in exchange for the dismantling of the Soviet missiles in Cuba. Kennedy decided to ignore the second message but to give a positive response to Khrushchev's offer. Khrushchev agreed to take the weapons out of Cuba, and an American invasion, scheduled for 29 October, was cancelled. 'The delicate and complex equilibrium of world power', or in other words, the nuclear status quo, was restored. Khrushchev took credit for preventing an invasion of Cuba; Kennedy took credit for standing up to the 'Russian Bear'. But the dangers of the Cold War were never so clearly demonstrated as during the Cuban crisis.

War in Vietnam
After the partitioning of Vietnam in 1954, the USA gave a great deal of aid, about US $250,000,000 per year, to the government of South Vietnam. The South's President, Ngo Dinh Diem, was an autocratic leader of a corrupt, repressive and basically unpopular regime. Yet, to the American public, South Vietnam was presented as 'Free Vietnam', and its president was 'the greatest little man in Asia'. As a London *Times* writer put it, his 'main supporters are to be found in North America, not in Free Vietnam'. Diem's support at home was primarily amongst the minority Catholic population and the wealthy land-owning class. All those who opposed Diem, whether communist or not, were ruthlessly dealt with. Nevertheless, opposition to Diem continued to grow, and amongst the peasantry in the villages, resistance strengthened under the leadership of the National Liberation Front.

The American military build-up in support of 'Free Vietnam' started to gather momentum in the early 1960s. Behind it lay the 'domino theory', which stated that the 'fall' of one state to communism would

Vietnamese civilians, mostly women and children, shelter from bombing by US planes. Even today the tragedy of Vietnam lives on in the United States' conscience.

swiftly be followed by the fall of neighbouring states. In Asia, the initial push was assumed to come from China. Hundreds of thousands of US troops were committed to the struggle against 'communist insurgency' and before long, the conflict in Vietnam had escalated to a war of almost genocidal proportions. A remark by one US soldier hints at the overall strategy: 'In order to protect this village,' he said, 'it will first be necessary to destroy it.' But US tactics, including massive bombing of the North, and of neighbouring Cambodia and Laos, and the use of chemical weapons against vast tracts of North Vietnamese territory, proved strategically futile. Ultimately, the Vietnamese would inflict on the USA its first bitter experience of military defeat.

7 DISSENTING OPINIONS

'The British people are prepared to be blown to atomic dust if necessary.' So said the Foreign Secretary at the height of the Berlin crisis, in 1961. Had they been consulted, many of the British people might have denied the fact. But, as regards nuclear policy in general there was little consultation with the public. Decisions affecting whole populations were made in secret by a small number of top politicians and military strategists. Concern at the prospect of nuclear annihilation prompted the formation of a number of protest groups in the 1950s. In Britain, these eventually came together around the Campaign for Nuclear Disarmament (CND).

Dupes of Moscow?
In 1955, eleven of the world's most eminent scientists, including Albert Einstein, issued a manifesto stressing the 'perils of nuclear war'. The manifesto concluded by posing two basic alternatives: 'Shall we put an end to the human race: or shall mankind renounce war?' One of its supporters, the philosopher and social critic Bertrand Russell, became the first president of CND, which was launched in February 1958. Another founder member, the novelist J. B. Priestley, wrote in CND's 'Statement of Policy' of 'the hysterical fear that is behind the arms race'. Britain, shortly beforehand, had exploded its first H-bomb, but, said the statement 'Britain cannot be adequately defended by atomic armaments. To retain them ... is merely to play an idiotic game of bluff.' CND urged unilateral nuclear disarmament by Britain, as the first step in a world-wide effort to 'ban the Bomb'.

'The matter ... transcends Party politics and even national boundaries,' wrote Russell. He argued against the view that it was better 'to have the human race destroyed than to have it succumb to communism', a view commonly expressed as 'Better dead than Red'. CND was sometimes accused of being sympathetic to, or even funded by, the Soviet Union. But with well-attended and peaceful protest marches, meetings and co-ordinated acts of 'civil disobedience', the organization made the issue of nuclear weapons policy a subject of widespread public debate. Its supporters claimed some credit for influencing the Partial Test Ban Treaty of 1963, which put an end to above-ground nuclear

Massive increases in weaponry brought enormous increases in anti-nuclear protests in the 1980s.

In the 1960s 'Ban the Bomb' protests were widespread and frequent.
This protest took place in Trafalgar Square.

testing, with its associated dangers of radioactive 'fall-out' spreading through the atmosphere. After this, however, membership steadily declined. A revival of CND, together with new forms of protest, was to take place only in the 1980s, by which time the 'nuclear threat' had increased dramatically.

American Antagonists

With the election of Kennedy as President of the US in 1960, nuclear policy in the United States underwent some change. No longer, as had been the case during the Eisenhower years, did the US rely on a threat of 'massive retaliation' against any state that attacked an American ally. Kennedy's policy was one of 'flexible response', or 'suitable, selective, swift and effective' action which need not involve the use of nuclear weapons. Yet the Cuban crisis had shown that certain situations were still capable of leading to all-out war between the super-powers. Following the decline of McCarthyism there was a rising swell of popular dissent in the US, as in Western Europe, against the dangers of the Cold War.

During the 1960s 'folk culture' gave a forum for some of the most significant opposition to the Cold War. Pete Seeger and Joan Baez were two of the best-known singers; another was Bob Dylan. In

Joan Baez in Trafalgar Square: 'folk culture' was a significant source of protest in the early 1960s.

'Flower power' was one form of reaction to the warmongering of the 'cold warriors'.

alternatively humorous, scathing, and ironic songs, Dylan denounced the 'cold warriors'. Hollywood emerged from the McCarthy years with a number of thought-provoking films.

Kennedy's assassination in November 1963 shocked the world. There remain many unanswered questions connected with it. Some of these tend to implicate extreme right-wing factions in the US who believed him to be 'soft on communism'. In a highly conciliatory speech, he had emphasized the common humanity of the American and Soviet peoples, called for a re-examination of American attitudes, and spoken of the absolute need to avoid war. It seems quite possible that, despite his record in general, Kennedy was a victim of Cold War ideology: a victim, not of the communists, but of those who, theoretically, sought most vigorously to uphold the values of the West. Possibly, however, such suggestions are only part of the continuing 'communist plot' to undermine the West. In the Cold War, 'propaganda' and 'truth' can sometimes mean the same thing.

Against the Party line
The Soviet leader, Khrushchev, personally authorized publication of a novel by Alexander Solzhenitsyn called *One Day in the Life of Ivan Denisovitch*. It was an account of the Gulag labour camps, where the author had been imprisoned for eight years during Stalin's time. However, this did not mark a long-term relaxation of censorship. In the USSR, 'dissident' opinions were rarely tolerated.

Khrushchev's policy of 'peaceful coexistence' with the West was condemned by the Chinese as 'revisionist' or, altering orthodox policies. 'The seizure of political power by the proletariat,' The Chinese *People's Daily* insisted, '... is accompanied invariably by the power of the gun.' But Khrushchev aimed to compete economically with capitalist Europe, and to await the legitimate election of Communist Party

'The Conference Excuses Itself'. A cartoon by Sir David Low, satirizing the failure of the superpowers to reach any peace agreements. The relevance of the cartoon has not been diminished over the years.

53

Alexander Solzhenitsyn, the exiled Soviet novelist, whose works are critical of the injustices of the Soviet regime. He was imprisoned and then exiled to Siberia before being deported to the West in 1974. He won the Nobel Prize for literature in 1970.

governments where, in France and Italy at least, this looked a real possibility. Periods of heightened tension between the USSR and China, and intermittent clashes on the borders of the two countries, sometimes threatened to escalate to war. The Chinese–Soviet dispute continued long after Nikita Khrushchev's removal from office, in 1964. 1964 was also the year China carried out its first atomic test, and with France having done so in 1960, there were now five nations with nuclear armouries.

The beginnings of a more rational relationship between the USSR and the West began to appear during the mid-1960s. A telephone link between Moscow and Washington, called the 'hot-line', had reduced the risk of misunderstandings that might lead to war. And in 1966 and 1967, Britain and France signed statements with the USSR stressing the importance of co-operation and a reduction of tension in Europe. In 1968, however, Soviet-led forces intervened in Czechoslovakia to overthrow the popular liberalizing government led by Alexander Dubcek. 'We cannot agree to have hostile forces push your country off the road to socialism ...' a Warsaw Pact note had informed him. This was reminiscent of Hungary in 1956, but in Czechoslovakia, there was no armed uprising against the tanks and soldiers. Instead, the people met the Soviet forces with peaceful protest, verbal argument and scorn. Dubcek's reforms were reversed, and the 'Prague Spring' was over. But the seeds of East–West 'détente' (the relaxing of tension) survived: there were signs of a thaw in the air.

A young Czech girl shouts at the Russian soldiers sitting on their tank in Prague on 26 August 1968, surrounded by sympathetic listeners. In Czechoslovakia there was no armed uprising against the Russians.

8 DÉTENTE: THE TEMPORARY THAW

Détente between East and West gave rise to contact and co-operation in a number of areas. It also gave rise to treaties of mutual recognition, trade agreements, cultural exchanges, and negotiations on arms-control. To many people, it seemed as if the Cold War was coming to an end. Meanwhile, however, new forms of weapons, and new nuclear strategies, were taking shape. '*Détente*', President Nixon warned the American Congress in 1973, 'is not the same as lasting peace.'

The German initiative
Behind *détente* lay a series of agreements concerning Germany. From 1966, when Willy Brandt became Foreign Minister, the West German government operated a new policy towards the Eastern bloc. This was called '*Ostpolitik*'. It acknowledged that, for the foreseeable future,

The first seeds of détente *were sown in 1959 when Khrushchev visited Washington. He is pictured here with Vice-President Nixon.*

East German leader Willy Brandt, pictured here paying tribute to the Jewish insurgents killed by the Nazis during the Jewish Ghetto Uprising in 1943.

German reunification was unlikely, and it aimed for an improvement in relations between West Germany and the countries of Eastern Europe. A solution to the 'Germany problem' seemed to be in sight. And if the FDR and the DDR could achieve a working relationship, it would do a great deal to stabilize the 'balance of power' in Europe. But for *Ostpolitik* to succeed, there had to be a general willingness to reduce tension throughout the continent. Accordingly, Brandt stated his support for troop reductions in Europe and for moves against the further spread of nuclear weapons.

One of Brandt's first acts as Chancellor, in 1969, was to sign the nuclear 'Non-Proliferation Treaty' (NPT). This treaty was intended to prevent the international spread of nuclear weapons technology, by preventing the transfer of information and hardware. It also committed the signatories (including the USA, Britain and the USSR) to progress on disarmament. To the Soviet Union, Brandt's signature was a token of genuine goodwill. Shortly afterwards, West Germany began to negotiate treaties of mutual respect and non-aggression with the USSR and Poland. Brandt simultaneously promoted moves towards a new Four Power agreement on Berlin.

By the end of 1970, as a leading British politician said, 'the whole situation in Europe had been transformed ... by Brandt's courage and vision.' The treaties with Poland and the USSR had been signed, and even more significantly, Brandt had twice had talks with the East German Prime Minister, Walter Ulbricht. The Berlin settlement of 1971 ensured a continuance of Four Power control and extended the rights of West Berliners to visit the East. Then, in December 1972, the 'two Germanies' signed a 'Basic Treaty'. It was not quite the same as full diplomatic recognition, but it guaranteed 'good neighbourly' relations, opening the way to a wide range of contacts. International recognition for both German states swiftly followed. *Ostpolitik* seemed to offer hope for a new realism in world affairs.

Strategic moves
Soon after becoming US President in 1969, Richard Nixon declared that the 'period of confrontation' between the superpowers was over. 'We shall enter into negotiation with the Soviet Union on a wide range of issues,' he informed his Nato allies. The following year, the USA and USSR began 'strategic arms limitation' (SALT) talks in Vienna.

'Strategic arms' consisted of long-range missiles and bombers, each equipped with a nuclear warhead. These systems had been developed during the late 1950s and early 1960s. They were associated with the theory of 'deterrence' or 'mutual assured destruction' ('MAD'). Promoters of this theory claimed that the threat of unacceptable retaliation prevented either side from starting a nuclear war. But the prevailing trend in the US, by 1970, was 'counterforce'. 'Counterforce' demanded comparatively new, highly accurate missile systems, which were capable of hitting specific military targets. It was a war-fighting stance and it included the possibility of a 'Multiple Independently-targetted Re-entry Vehicle' or 'MIRV', which carried not one but several warheads. The MIRV programme was not a part of the SALT negotiations, nor were the many 'tactical' weapons considered essential to any plans for 'limited nuclear war' in Europe, 'should deterrence fail'.

In April 1971, a United States table tennis team was invited to China. This led rapidly to a 'thaw' in US–Chinese relations, publicly symbolized by Nixon's visit to China the following February. A 'safer and better world' could be achieved, he said, 'if we have a strong, healthy United States, Europe, Soviet Union, China, Japan, each balancing the other ...' Then in May 1972, Nixon travelled to the USSR, and in Moscow he signed SALT I. This was an 'interim agreement' that

The 1970s saw an improvement in East–West relations. Here the Russian ballet dancer Mikhail Baryshnikov rehearses during a visit of the Bolshoi Ballet to the USA. (He later defected to the West.)

restricted the numbers of long-range missiles on both sides. But even at these levels, each side still had enough to destroy the other many times over. 'We have a two-to-one lead in missiles,' Nixon assured Congress the following year. '. . . I am determined that our military power will remain second to none.' *Pravda's* commentary on SALT I drew attention to the economic consequences of the arms race, as well as to its fundamental dangers: 'The agreements signed must promote the checking of the arms drive which creates the threat of a rocket-nuclear conflict, and diverts vast means from creative objectives.' But, with US 'counterforce' technology setting the pace, arms spending over the following decade would inevitably rise to new heights.

Members of the Chinese table tennis team, on a playing and sightseeing tour of the United States, applaud President Richard Nixon during a reception in the Rose Garden of the White House in 1972.

Leonid Brezhnev, Soviet First Secretary between 1964 and 1982, and Richard M. Nixon, US President 1969–74, pose for the cameras during détente.

Trust and respect

'The way to peace lies through exchange of ideas, through the free movement of individuals,' the French Foreign Minister stated in July 1973. At the Finnish capital, Helsinki, the 'European Security Conference' was under way. Its aim was to build trust, tolerance and mutual respect across Europe. Ultimately, perhaps, a comprehensive arrangement of non-aggression treaties could replace NATO and the Warsaw Pact. The USSR had pressed for such a system since the early 1950s, as it would decrease American influence on the continent. Now, from NATO's point of view, circumstances were favourable.

For three years or so, there had been growing political pressure in the USA for the withdrawal of troops from Europe. This had led the Western allies to seek negotiations with the Warsaw Pact on 'Mutual and Balanced Force Reductions'. Then, in January 1973, after ten years' disastrous involvement in Vietnam, the United States signed 'peace with honour', and the deeply detested 'draft', conscription into the US Armed Forces was abolished. The consequent lowering of US troop-levels, world-wide, increased the need for withdrawal of troops from Europe. With this added incentive for the West, 'force reduction' talks began in Vienna in October 1973. They were linked with the negotiations in Helsinki: progress or failure in Vienna could affect the outcome of Helsinki, and vice-versa.

Gerald Ford, who became President of the US in 1974, after Richard Nixon was forced to resign.

During a visit to the USA that year by the Soviet leader Leonid Brezhnev, he and President Nixon declared their joint commitment to policies designed 'to avoid military confrontation, and . . . to exclude the outbreak of nuclear war.' 'I am not dangerous', Brezhnev assured the American people. Shortly afterwards, in a series of television appearances, Nixon was assuring them, 'I am not a criminal'. It was the height of the 'Watergate scandal', which exposed corruption in some sectors of the American government. By August 1974, Nixon's credibility was completely shattered and he was facing impeachment procedures. There was no alternative to resignation, and he became the first US President to leave office in disgrace.

Nixon's successor, Gerald Ford, emphasized that there was 'no rational alternative to accords of mutual restraint' between the superpowers. A second round of SALT talks began in November 1974. Then, at Helsinki in August 1975, an agreement was signed. This contained recognition for East European borders, and also assurances from all participating nations concerning East–West communication and 'respect for human rights and fundamental freedoms'. As it turned out however, with the Helsinki Accords *détente* had reached its peak; the 'Second Cold War' was on its way.

9 DOWN TO ZERO

'The Second Cold War' refers to the period from the late 1970s to the present day, when various political, economic, social and military pressures combined to end *détente*. Jimmy Carter, the US President from 1977 to 1981, had the image of an easy-going, liberal peanut farmer. But amongst his predecessors, Carter most admired President Harry Truman. Perhaps then, in view of Truman's resolutely anti-Soviet record, it is not so surprising that the 'Second Cold War' should have had its origins in Carter's presidency. With the election of his successor, Ronald Reagan, hostility between the superpowers intensified to an alarming degree. As before, international and domestic events interacted, producing a chilling atmosphere of ideological confrontation. And as before, above it all loomed the ever-present, and possibly ever-increasing, danger of nuclear conflict.

Soviet President Leonid Brezhnev waves to the audience as US President Jimmy Carter smiles, shortly after both had signed the SALT II Treaty in 1979.

The Third World connection

Just before his death in the American-backed coup of 1973, Chile's democratically elected Marxist President, Salvador Allende, broadcast a final message to his supporters: 'Neither crime nor force are strong enough to hold back the process of social change,' he said. 'History belongs to us, because it is made by the people.' But to many American policy-makers, political and social revolution anywhere in the world signified 'Soviet expansionism'. A wave of revolutionary activity in the Third World between 1974 and 1980 seemed to confirm the view that, once again, the 'Soviet menace' was threatening international peace and stability. And yet, even amongst the US establishment, some opposed this view. The US Rear Admiral Gene La Roque said in 1980:

> 'It just baffles me how we have developed this paranoia about the Soviets. The Soviets are in six relatively unimportant countries today. They're in Angola, Mozambique, Ethiopia, Cuba, Afghanistan and South Yemen. ... I think our fear of the Soviets is based on lack of information and total absence of any factual data.'

The USSR sent 100,000 Soviet troops into Afghanistan in December 1979, having been asked by the Afghan government to help fight the rebels. The event was condemned by the UN and the West.

Carter's policy was to 'link' progress on *détente* to 'Soviet adventurism' abroad, to Eastern-bloc treatment of dissidents and Soviet policy towards Jewish emigration. The harsh suppression of East European groups and individuals, who sought full implementation of the Helsinki accords on 'human rights and fundamental freedoms, contributed substantially to the breakdown of *détente*.

The intervention of 100,000 Soviet troops in Afghanistan, beginning in December 1979, was roundly condemned in the UN by 'non-aligned' and Western nations alike. '*Détente* will not survive another shock of this order,' the French and West German leaders warned the Soviet leaders. The USSR claimed that it had been called upon by the revolutionary government of Afghanistan to assist it against a Muslim 'counter-revolution'. But before long, the war against the Afghan guerrillas seemed to have become as disastrous a venture for the USSR as war against communism in Indo-China had been for the USA. And ironically, the USSR was fighting the same 'Islamic fundamentalism' (belief in the absolute authority of the Islamic religion) that had overthrown the USA's ally, the Shah of Iran, in January 1979. The year-long 'Iranian hostage crisis' which followed that, and the bungled US attempt to rescue the captive Americans, contributed greatly to a sense of national failure and weakness in the USA. It was the demand for a stronger and more assertive America that led directly to Ronald Reagan's election, late in 1980.

Echoes of the past

'I will not stand by and watch this country destroy itself under mediocre leadership that drifts from one crisis to the next, eroding our national will.' With his vision of the nation as a 'shining city on a hill', Reagan caught the voters' mood, which was nostalgia for a 'former glory' and eager longing for a return to international pre-eminence.

In Poland, popular pressure had led to the creation of a free trade-union, Solidarity. The union's demand for far-reaching political and social reforms led, in December 1981, to the imposition of martial law in Poland. Had this not happened, there was every likelihood of direct intervention by Warsaw Pact forces, as had happened in Hungary and Czechoslovakia in previous years. The subsequent suppression of Solidarity proved, once again, the impossibility of liberalization in Eastern Europe.

A number of spy cases, defections and 'secrets' trials, revived other memories of the earlier cold war. Most spectacular, from the British public's point of view, was the exposure of the Keeper of the Queen's Pictures, art-historian Anthony Blunt, as a former spy (the mysterious 'fourth man' of the Philby–Burgess–Maclean network). Spies from East Germany were also found to have penetrated to the highest levels

Lech Walesa, leader of the Polish trade union Solidarity, *pictured outside union headquarters in Gedansk.*

of West German government service.

American right-wing politicians could never fully accept the policy of diplomacy with the East. One commentator denounced what he called 'sickly inhibitions against the use of military force'. It was clear that many of Reagan's supporters expected him to take some action, somewhere, to enforce the 'national will'.

Two revolutionary regimes in Central America, Grenada and Nicaragua, received particular attention. Both were considered to be 'satellite' states of Cuba. In 1984, a US-led invasion force 'liberated' Grenada, apparently to the relief of most of the population. Had Reagan chosen to invade Nicaragua too, US forces would certainly have been strongly resisted.

In Nicaragua, the Sandinista revolution of 1979 had overthrown the US-supported dictatorship of the Somoza family and introduced genuinely popular reforms. The US considered direct invasion to be problematic, and instead gave massive support, economically and militarily, to the anti-Sandinista guerrilla forces, the Contras. In neighbouring Honduras, American military advisors are still training the Contras in methods of destabilization and selective assassination.

A question of survival
'We fought World War I in Europe, we fought World War II in Europe and if you dummies let us, we'll fight World War III in Europe.' Admiral La Roque's warning came as quite a shock to most people. Whatever happened to 'deterrence'? Wasn't World III 'unthinkable'? Apparently not: Jimmy Carter's 'Presidential Directive No 59' (1980) confirmed the shift in US military planning. 'The possibility of fighting a nuclear war, lasting weeks or even months, is envisaged.' 'Counterforce', suddenly, was public knowledge and the new 'generation' of

United States troops in Grenada, 1983.

A new form of permanent protest began with the Women's Peace Camp outside the US Airforce base at Greenham Common in England.

US/NATO weaponry was scheduled for deployment (use) almost immediately.

Many West Europeans were appalled by the implications of this, and there was a rapid growth in the 'peace movement' during the early 1980s. The British Prime Minister, Margaret Thatcher, was one of the most stridently anti-Soviet Western leaders, and her government was determined to 'modernize' the British nuclear armoury. The 'Polaris' submarine fleet would be replaced with the new 'Trident' system, which involved a tenfold increase in the number of warheads. New 'Cruise' missiles would also be stationed in Britain. Large-scale protests by the massively-increased membership of CND, and vigorous opposition by smaller groups such as the peace camps outside various missile bases seemed to have little impact on government policy. Nor did such well-publicized statements as that made by Lord Mountbatten: 'In the event of nuclear war . . . there will be no survivors—all will be obliterated. . . . The nuclear arms race has no military purpose. Wars cannot be fought with nuclear weapons.'

In West Germany, Holland, Belgium, the US and elsewhere, there were equally insistent, and apparently equally ineffectual, protests.

The 'European Nuclear Disarmament' organization attempted to link East and West on the issue, pressing for a 'nuclear-free zone' across the continent. But peace activists in Eastern Europe, predictably, were unable to criticize their own governments' policies. As always, the USSR was determined to keep pace with Western 'advances' in weaponry, despite the US ban on 'high-tech' exports.

'The deadly logic of self-destruction spares no expense,' the West German novelist Gunter Grass has said. The sheer cost of the arms build-up is staggering: for 1981–6, the US 'defense' budget was estimated at $1,600,000,000,000—and then revised upwards by up to fifty per cent.

Scientists have predicted the catastrophic effects on the environment of even a 'limited' nuclear conflict. They claim that so much dust and debris would rise into the atmosphere that the sun would be blotted out for months. In this 'Arctic night' all plant life would wither and perish. There would be no hope of survival, even for military and government leaders sitting out the conflict in their deep, bomb-resistant shelters. And it has often been pointed out that a failed 'silicon chip' in the computerized defences of either side could result in accidental nuclear war.

Third World famine and poverty is often contrasted with the vast sums spent on armaments by the superpowers.

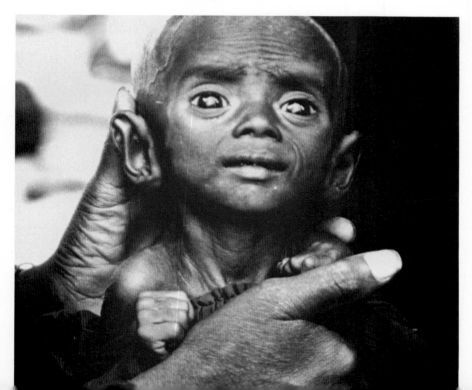

Nuclear war would mean widespread devastation, on a scale even greater than that experienced by Hiroshima in 1945.

In 1983 came President Reagan's 'Strategic Defense Initiative'. Popularly known as 'Star Wars', this envisaged a world at last 'free from the threat of nuclear war'. Space-based laser systems would destroy enemy missiles before they reached their targets; supposedly, it would be a perfect 'defensive shield' against attack. But was it realistically feasible? Many experts denounced it as unworkable, others, as an irresponsible fantasy. The new Soviet First Secretary, Mikhail Gorbachev, said in 1985: 'This project will, no doubt, whip up the arms race in all areas, which means that the threat of war will increase. That is why this project is bad for us and for you and for everybody in general.'

Speaking of the Soviet and American peoples, prior to the Geneva summit of November 1985 when he met with President Reagan, Gorbachev insisted, 'Whether we like one another or not, we can either survive or perish only together.' Nothing of substance was agreed, but further meetings between the American and Soviet leaders were fixed for 1986 and 1987. Could this be the beginning of the end of the Cold War?

GLOSSARY

Accord   Agreement.

Autocratic   A form of rule which is dictatorial and absolute.

Bloc   A group of countries combined by a common interest or aim.

Bolshevik   The 'majority' or 'extreme' faction of the Russian Social Democratic Party, which was renamed 'Communist' soon after the Revolution.

Capitalism   An economic and social system based on the right of private businesses to own and control the means of producing and distributing goods.

Class struggle   A politically motivated conflict between different social and economic groupings, such as between the 'proletariat' (working class) and the 'bourgeoisie' (middle class), or between peasants and land-owners.

Colonial   Where representatives of an occupying power rule a country.

Communism   An economic and social system based on common ownership and control of the means of producing and distributing goods.

Constitutional   According to the supreme law of the state.

Containment   A principle of US foreign policy that seeks to prevent the expansion of communist power.

Defection   A change of loyalty such as from the communist system to the capitalist system, which involves being exiled from one's homeland.

Détente   The relaxing of tension between nations.

Dissident   Someone who disagrees with his or her government's actions or policies.

Enclave   A part of a country entirely surrounded by foreign territory.

Fascism   An anti-communist and racist theory of politics and social organization which encourages militarism and state power.

Fifth column   An organization of spies, saboteurs etc, who work behind enemy lines.

Genocidal   The policy of deliberately killing a nationality or race.

Guerrilla   A form of warfare conducted by small, mobile bands of troops against a regular army.

Ideology   A body of ideas that reflect the beliefs and interests of a nation or political system.

Imperialism   The dominance of one nation by another through military, economic or cultural expansion.

Insurgency   A rebellion or uprising against the established authorities.

Marxist–Leninist   Concerning the principles of Karl Marx as interpreted, developed and applied by Lenin (1870–1924).

Non-aligned state   A nation which carries out policies independent of the super-powers.

Power-vacuum   A situation in which there is no obvious or settled authority.

Proletariat   The class of wage earners in a capitalist society.

Propaganda   Information which is designed to promote or undermine a particular cause or belief.

Radioactive fall-out   The dust from a nuclear explosion which gives off fatal invisible rays.

Red-baiting   The taunting and persecution of supposed communists.

Red Scare   A period of apprehension and paranoia, concerning the expansion of communism in the West.

Revisionist   Tending to alter and revise orthodox theories.

Satellite state   A nation which is dependent upon another for economic support and political direction.

Smear tactics   Damaging allegations intended to associate an individual with dubious activities or beliefs.

Socialism   An economic and social system based on state ownership and control of the means of producing and distributing goods.

Soviet Presidium   The permanent committee of the Soviet government.

Subversion   The overthrow or destruction of established authority.

Totalitarian   Where every aspect of life comes under the control of central state authority.

Vietminh   A Vietnamese organization led by Ho Chi Minh that first fought the Japanese and then the French (1941–54) in an attempt to achieve national independence.

PICTURE ACKNOWLEDGEMENTS

Camerapress 10, (Ritchie), 16, 20, 22, 30 (Curtis/RBO), 34 (Dalmas), 49 (Lennox Smillie), 61, 64 (Barrie Penrose), 68; Hutchison Library COVER (right); Imperial War Museum 7; Sir David Low (Evening Standard) 53; Popperfoto 26, 27, 40, 51, 52, 57, 70; Topham COVER (left), 4, 5, 8, 9, 11, 12, 18, 21, 24, 25, 28, 29, 32, 33, 36, 37, 38, 39, 41, 42, 43, 44, 45, 47, 50, 54, 55, 56, 59, 62, 63, 66, 67; Malcolm S. Walker 17; Wayland Picture Library 13, 14, 23, 60, 69.

DATE CHART

1945 Defeat of Nazi
Germany: spheres of
influence start to take
shape in Europe.
Atom-bombing of
Hiroshima and Nagasaki
ends Second World War

1946 Churchill's 'iron curtain'
speech.

1947 Truman Doctrine and
Marshall Plan
announced.

1948 Start of Berlin blockade
and airlift: ends 1949.

1949 Formation of NATO.

1950 Korean War begins.

1953 Death of Stalin.
Berlin uprising.
End of Korean War.
USSR tests H-bomb.

1955 West Germany joins
NATO.
Formation of Warsaw
Pact.
Scientists appeal against
nuclear weapons.

1956 Khrushchev denounces
Stalin, announces
'peaceful coexistence'.
Hungarian Uprising.
Suez.

1958 Soviet pressure over
Berlin.
Formation of CND.

1959 Victory of Cuban
Revolution.
Khrushchev visits USA.

1961 Bay of Pigs invasion
(Cuba).
Kennedy/Khrushchev
summit.
Berlin Wall erected.

1962 US troops build-up
underway in Vietnam.
Cuban missile crisis.

1963 Kennedy assassinated.
Partial Test Ban Treaty.

1964 Khrushchev deposed.
China tests A-bomb.

1966 Beginnings of *Ostpolitik*.

1968 'Prague Spring': Soviet-
led invasion of
Czechoslovakia.

1969 Nixon becomes US
President.
Beginnings of *détente*.

1970 SALT talks start.

1971	Four-Power agreement on Berlin.	**1979**	Islamic Revolution in Iran: US hostages seized. Nicaraguan revolution. Soviet forces intervene in Afghanistan.
1972	Nixon visits China and the USSR. SALT 1 signed		
1973	Helsinki talks begin. Allende overthrown in Chile. Vietnam armistice. Brezhnev visits USA.	**1984**	'Star Wars' research under way. US-led invasion of Grenada.
1974	Nixon resigns. India tests A-bomb.	**1985**	Gorbachev becomes Soviet First Secretary. Reagan/Gorbachev summit.
1975	Helsinki agreement.		

FURTHER READING

General accounts:
Baker, Elizabeth *The Cold War* (Wayland 1972)
Bown, Colin & Mooney, Peter J. *Cold War to Détente 1945–1980* (Heinemann 1981)
Halliday, Fred *The Making of the Second Cold War* (Verso/NLB 1983)
Higgins, Hugh *The Cold War* (Heinemann 1974)
McCauley, Martin *The Origins of the Cold War* (Longman 1983)

Documentary and related material:
Brown, Anthony Cave & MacDonald, Charles B. *On a Field of Red* (Putnams 1981)
Ceplair, Larry & Englund, Steven *The Inquisition in Hollywood* (Anchor Press/Doubleday 1980)
Minnion, John & Bolsover, Philip (ed.) *The CND Story* (Alison & Busby 1983)
Prins, Gwyn (ed.) *Defended to Death* (Penguin 1983)
Schell, Jonathan *The Fate of the Earth* (Picador 1982)

INDEX

Hoxha, President 12
HUAC 26, 28
Hungary 37–9, 55, 65

Kennedy, John F. 43, 44, 46,
  50, 51, 52
Khrushchev, Nikita 34, 35, 36,
  39, 41, 42, 43, 46, 53, 54
Kremlin 35

Maclean, Donald 30, 31, 65
Mao Tse-tung, Chairman 18, 19
Marshall Plan 15
Marx, Karl 6, 8, 18
McCarthy, Senator Joseph 25,
  26, 29, 31, 51, 52

Nagasaki 4, 9
Nasser, President 37
NATO 32, 33, 35, 58, 61, 68
Ngo Dinh Diem, President 46
Nicaragua 67
Nixon, Richard 56, 58
Nuclear weapons 33, 43, 44, 51,
  57, 68

Oppenheimer, Robert 9
Ospolitik 56, 57, 58

Philby, Kim 31, 65
Poland 57, 65
Pravda 15, 60
Priestly, J. B. 48

Reagan, Ronald, President 63.
  65, 66, 67, 70
'Red-baiting' 28–9, 72
Revisionist 35, 53, 72
Roosevelt, Theodore 5

Rosenberg, Julius and Ethel 29,
  31

SALT talks 58, 60, 62
Socialism 6, 19, 38, 55, 72
Solidarity 65
Solzhenitsyn, Alexander 53, 54
Stalin, Joseph 5, 8, 11, 12, 13,
  35, 36, 38, 53
'Star Wars' 70
Suez crisis 37–9

Thatcher, Margaret, Prime
  Minister 68
Third World 18–24, 64
Tito, Marshal 12, 35
Treaty
  Austrian State 35
  Non-Proliferation 57
Truman Doctrine 15
Truman, Harry 12, 14, 15, 17,
  19, 32

Ulbricht, Walter 40, 41, 58
United Nations 10, 19

Vietminh 22
Vietnam 22, 45, 46–7

Walesa, Lech 66
War
  First World 67
  Greek civil 15
  Korean 19, 20, 33
  Nuclear 5, 48, 58, 67, 69
  Second World 4, 8, 11, 67
  Vietnam 46–7
Warsaw Pact 35, 39, 43, 55, 61
Watergate 62
'Witch hunts' 25–7